About the Front Cover

The road repair scene is a metaphor. Christ's cross stands
site and illustrates His healing power over our wounded world. The pool of Christ's blood at the foot of the cross, relates to the assurance of faith God wants to give us, that our hearts are sprinkled to cleanse us from a guilty conscience as well as the forgiveness of our sins (Hebrews 10v22). He is the Son of "I AM – Jehovah, Almighty God" of Exodus 3v14 in the Bible. He IS Love and powerful to redeem mankind from sin. He beckons us to joyfully receive spiritual rebirth and follow His narrow, holy, road from death to life.

The narrow and wide gates

"Enter through the narrow gate. For wide is the gate and broad is the road that leads to destruction, and many enter through it. But small is the gate and narrow the road that leads to life, and only a few find it." (Matthew 7v13-14)

ISBN 978-0-9927570-2-1

Dedicated to

Jesus Christ my Lord and Saviour,
to Rosemary my wife, and to the memory of the late Terry Daly who encouraged me to trust in the love of Christ as recorded in the Bible promises of Ephesians 3v16-21:

"I pray that out of his glorious riches he may strengthen you with power through his Spirit in your inner being, so that Christ may dwell in your hearts through faith. And I pray that you, being rooted and established in love, may have power together with all the saints, to grasp how long and wide and high and deep is the love of Christ, and to know this love that surpasses knowledge – that you may be filled to the measure of the fullness of God."

"Now to him who is able to do immeasurably more than we ask or imagine, according to his power that is at work within us, to him be glory in the church and in Christ Jesus throughout all generations, for ever and ever! Amen"

God is inviting us to continually pray for greater and deeper understanding of His love for us as individuals.

Acknowledgements

I am grateful to Mark Porthouse, my IT support and publishing facilitator and to Christian friends, Mathew Backholer editor and publisher, Rob Spiller, Eric Holdstock, Brian and Mary Smith, Stephanie Horlock and Rosemary my wife for their wisdom, experience and proofreading.

As author of this book, I, David Dare, take full responsibility for its contents.

Table of Contents

Introduction

My personal Journey from Death to Life has involved various questions and experiences. The following examples, with notes following, may encourage your own thoughts about this life and beyond. Select any one that is of particular interest to you:

1. Where might I find guidance about life after death? (p9)
2. Is there a 'yardstick' against which I might measure my life? (p15)
3. How did sin and evil in the world originate and how does God overcome them on our behalf? (p21)
4. Who has the power to guide me safely through this journey from death to life? (p29)
5. Can one know Jesus personally as compared to just knowing about him? (p33)
6. What would be expected of me in following Jesus? (p39)
7. How would I maintain this new, personal faith? (p45)

Firstly – For the benefit of any reader who is unfamiliar with Christianity, one encounters the mystery of God – Father, Son and Holy Spirit, full of love and grace towards mankind, building God's everlasting kingdom/church on Earth as follows:

- Jesus Christ, its great teacher is The Son of God who left His glory in Heaven to become our saviour on Earth followed by his resurrection and return to Heaven. “Blessed are those who mourn for they will be comforted.” (Matthew 5v4).
- In acknowledging our spiritual poverty and accepting God’s salvation in Jesus Christ, we can receive God’s gracious, free gift of faith and receive God’s forgiveness. His Holy Spirit enables us to understand the Bible (Ephesians 2v8-9).
- Christ then dwells in us – a “mystery that has been kept hidden for ages and generations, but is now disclosed to the Lord’s people. To them God has chosen to make known among the Gentiles the glorious riches of this mystery, which is Christ in you, the hope of glory.” (Colossians 1v26-27). Getting to know Jesus helps us gain His qualities in our daily lives in His church and kingdom on Earth.

God’s Mysteries

All the foregoing is part of the divine mystery of how it was necessary for Christ to bear away our sins through His own death on our behalf. Through His prophet Isaiah he says “my thoughts are not your thoughts, neither are your ways my ways.”declares the lord, “as the heavens are higher than the earth, so are my ways higher than your ways and my thoughts than your thoughts.” (Isaiah 55v8-9)

How does history record God's dealings with mankind?

This history or, if you like, "His-Story" is as follows:

Around 4,000 years ago, God challenged one person named Abram, then living in today's Mesopotamia, to leave his settled state and move with his family to a place God would show him. God promised he would become a nation that would bless the world and also that God would provide his own family with a land in which to live – today's Israel.

That land was given to Abram, Isaac and Jacob, the "Promised Land". Abram believed God and "It was accounted to him as Righteousness". Later, God changed Abram's name to Abraham.

Abraham had a son Isaac and a grandson Jacob who became the father of the twelve tribes of Israel. God allowed them to be slaves in Egypt for 400 years during which they grew to a million people. Some 3500 years ago, God sent His servant Moses to rescue them and gave them – and us – the code of conduct for the whole of humanity – the Ten Commandments as listed later in this booklet.

Two thousand years ago, Israel would birth the Messiah (saviour), God's own son, Jesus Christ of a virgin in Bethlehem. God's Holy Spirit, in turn, birthed His kingdom on earth – His church which, since then, has been the vehicle through which God's 'Good News'/Gospel, has been reaching the rest of us globally.

The prophet Isaiah explains how God's thoughts and ways are different to ours (Isaiah 55v8-9). The Apostle Paul, four times, describes these 'Eternal purposes of God' as intellectually mysterious (Ephesians 3v1-10). But God has chosen HIS times for each step to happen (Galatians 4v4).

1. Where might I find guidance about life after death?

Answer: The Bible e.g.:

"All Scripture is God-breathed and is useful for teaching, rebuking, correcting and training in righteousness" (2 Tim 3v16), "Just as man is destined to die once, and after that to face judgment, so Christ was sacrificed once to take away the sins of many people; and he will appear a second time, not to bear sin, but to bring salvation to those who are waiting for him" (Hebrews 9v27-28)

"For the word of God is alive and active. Sharper than any double-edged sword, it penetrates even to dividing soul and spirit, joints and marrow; it judges the thoughts and attitudes of the heart. Nothing in all creation is hidden from God's sight. Everything is uncovered and laid bare before the eyes of him to whom we must give account." (Hebrews 4v12-13) The Christian Faith involves us reading and meditating on His word with childlike trust. It then daily becomes "a lamp for my feet, a light on my path." (Psalm 119v105). The following anecdote illustrates this truth:

The Pacific Islander and "the wood that talked"

It was 1850, no writing of any kind was known to the inhabitants of the New Hebrides islands in the Pacific Ocean. Missionary John Paton needed some nails and tools from his ship moored off shore. He pencilled a few words on a piece of planed wood and asked the islander to take it to his wife who was on the ship. In blank wonder the islander had stared at him and said "But what do you want?" He replied, "The wood will tell her." As he set off, the Islander had angrily muttered "Whoever heard of wood talking."

On his return, the Islander brought back the bit of wood with the supplies and made signs for an explanation. With his best attempt at the local language, John translated the words on the wood for him and informed him that in the same way, God speaks to us through His book the Bible. The will of God was written there and, by and by, when the islander learned to read, he would hear God speaking to him from its pages just as his wife had heard John from the wood.

The Bible was written by God-inspired men over the ages. By humbly reading it, we gradually gain the heartfelt assurance of God's purposes for our lives here – and in eternity. Its main objective is to help us to know and trust God's Son, Jesus Christ.

The boyhood conversion of my brother-in-law, Kenneth Durman

Photograph: Taken while serving with Rhodesian forces during the Second World War.

Easter Sunday, April 7th 1927, aged seven, in Ken's own words.

Setting: Ken's bedroom in the superintendent's apartment attached to the Salvation Army, Men's hostel on Burne Street, just off the Edgware Road in London.

Recalling the occasion, Ken, in his own words, remembers – It was the most important evening of my life: sleep did not come and my mind wandered through the various homilies I had heard in church that day. Death and eternal life are key aspects of Easter and, suddenly, I realised I was mortal and would face death one day. This was frightening and I knew I should accept Christ because His supreme sacrifice has purchased our forgiveness, and His resurrection has brought us the gift of eternal life. But what should I say in prayer to accept all this? It was a terrifying dilemma. Just as I reached this point in my thoughts, I heard the rattle of the keys of the hostel's night watchman as he came into our tiny, concrete paved back yard to check that all was well there. Quickly, before he moved away, I got out of bed and hurried to slide up the back window of my bedroom. I called down with a panicky voice, "Get my father to come here quickly!" The man asked, "What's the matter?" but I repeated the request (that sounded like an order) to hurry and get my father. The service in the hostel was still in progress and a visiting preacher was in the middle of his sermon. The night watchman's urgent beckoning brought my father off the podium and to the back of the hall. The urgency in my voice had made the man think there must be a fire or something equally dire.

Dad came rushing in and upstairs to my room. By then I was back in bed. He asked "What's the matter, son?" "I want to get saved," I said. Then and there, he explained and made sure I understood what I was asking; then, guided by him, I prayed the penitent's prayer and accepted Jesus as my Saviour. What a relief it was! I went to sleep with peace in my heart. How wonderful it is that God does not specify the reason we should have for seeking him; just that we should seek Him in sincerity and truth.

Example of a penitent's prayer.

Believe that you are a sinner and pray "Dear God I admit that I have done many things that displease you. I am sorry. I believe Jesus died that I can be forgiven. Please forgive me and come into my life and help me to live your way.

2. Is there a 'yardstick' against which I might measure my life?

Answer: The Bible tells us that we all fall short of the glory of God. This is caused by sin which separates us from God's love. God's word reveals where we individually fail. Also, that if we admit and repent (turn away from) our sin, He is faithful and just to forgive us through the substitutionary sacrifice of His only Son, Jesus the perfect "**LAMB OF GOD** who takes away the sin of the world" (John 1v29).

He gave His Ten Commandments to Moses on Mount Sinai as 'bench-marks' for our behaviour. They are also the basis of much law today. Examining these, we soon see why the Bible says that "We all, like sheep have gone astray, each of us has turned to our own way" (Isaiah 53:6). It is the law, that shows us our failings.

We simply apply all this by repenting of our sins and receiving God's gift of grace by believing in His love for mankind. In so doing, death, the wages of sin, are exchanged for the gift of eternal life through our Lord Jesus Christ. It is not through our good works but through our entire reliance on God and **faith in him**.

Just as Christ rose from the dead, we too can eventually be raised to eternal life with Christ – see John chapter 6. In the meantime, we can experience "God in us, our hope of glory" (Colossians 1v27).

The Ten Commandments (from Exodus 20 and Deuteronomy 5)

1. You shall have no other gods before me.

2. You shall not make for yourself an image in the form of anything in heaven above or on the earth beneath or in the waters below. You shall not bow down to them or worship them.

3. You shall not misuse the name of the Lord your God.

4. Remember the Sabbath day by keeping it holy.

5. Honour your father and your mother.

6. You shall not murder.

7. You shall not commit adultery.

8. You shall not steal.

9. You shall not give false testimony against your neighbour.

10. You shall not covet your neighbour's house. You shall not covet your neighbour's wife, nor his male or female servant, his ox or donkey, or anything that belongs to your neighbour.

Realising that mankind cannot keep all these commandments, Jesus said, “A new command I give you: love one another. As I have loved you, so you must love one another.” John 13v34.

“So in everything, do to others what you would have them do to you, for this sums up the Law and the Prophets.” Matthew 7v12.

The following story of Paul Lennox is relevant:

Idi Amin and the death of my close friend Paul Lennox

In 1960s Uganda, I experienced the danger of having anything to do with the infamous President Idi Amin, who was associated with the death of my close friend Paul Lennox. That would be some forty years before writing this memoir. I soon realised that telling others the Gospel of Christ could involve spiritual opposition but, at the same time, it could be 'underwritten' by God's promise in Isaiah 55 that "His word will not return void." This principle has held true throughout my Christian life.

During a stopover in Nairobi en-route to the Seychelles in the mid 1970s, I was entertained to supper by charter pilot Paul Lennox (pictured left) and his wife Sheila during which I shared my testimony of having accepted Christ as my Saviour and Lord. Paul dropped me off at my hotel, at which point we paused as I asked Paul where he stood spiritually. Of all my friends, Paul was a man of exceptional integrity so I was not surprised when he said he wanted to make his peace with God. He declined my offer to lead him in prayer and he simply prayed for forgiveness and invited Christ into his life as Saviour and Lord.

Shortly after this, Paul was hired to fly two businessmen to Entebbe, Uganda to meet President Amin with Paul not realising that they were military arms dealers. While Paul's aircraft was parked at Entebbe airport, rival arms dealers placed an altitude bomb in Paul's plane which exploded as Paul descended to land back at Nairobi killing Paul and his passengers. Sheila telephoned me with this awful news and I returned to Nairobi to pay tribute to Paul at his funeral and share Paul's recent surrender to Christ and my personal assurance that he was safe with God.

In retelling that story now, I have remembered Paul's actual words of confession which were simply:

"Lord, forgive me that I have not loved you as I should."

The Gospel of Luke 23v39-43 describes how one of the two criminals crucified with Jesus feared God and said "Jesus remember me when you come into your kingdom" Jesus answered him "I tell you the truth, today you will be with me in paradise." How wonderful that we can be assured that my friend Paul met his Saviour before he died.

All this is "the mystery that has been kept hidden for ages and generations, but is now disclosed to the Lord's people. To them God has chosen to make known among the Gentiles the glorious riches of this mystery, which is Christ in you, the hope of glory." (Colossians 1v26-27).

The 'Born Again' Experience involves us reflecting on our past life in the light of God's word. That is when the Holy Spirit can help us to move our appreciation of God's love for us "from our head to our heart".

3. How did sin and evil in the world originate and how does God overcome them on our behalf?

Answer: In Luke 10v18, Jesus said "***I SAW** Satan fall like lightning from heaven*"

Revelation 12v7-9 records how "There was war in heaven. Michael and his angels fought against the dragon, and the dragon and his angels fought back. But he was not strong enough, and they lost their place in heaven. The great dragon was hurled down – that ancient serpent called the devil, or Satan, who leads the whole world astray. He was hurled to the earth, and his angels with him." but, we are also told that "Jesus came to destroy the works of the devil."

To dispel any doubt as to the truth of this scripture, Christ's own, threefold temptation by Satan is recorded in Matthew 3v1-11 as revealed by The Holy Spirit of God.

To enable Him to forgive our own sins, God protects the integrity of His righteous and holy universal law, by bearing His wrath against sin himself and this through the suffering of His only beloved son, our Lord Jesus Christ.

Hebrews 1v2-3 identifies Christ as the creator and sustainer of the universe. Hebrews 2v8-10 confirms how He offered himself to cleanse us by His blood shed on the cross.

This is illustrated by the following story about my 1974, Bible College friend Nazmi:

The Nazmi Iraq story

Myself and Nazmi Iraq at the Bible College of Wales in 1974

College principal Mr Samuel, visited me one evening and asked me to take care of, and share my double room with, a refugee who had just arrived from Turkey with little English. It turned out that Nazmi was actually Kurdish and lived by the Turkish border in Iraq with his Roman Catholic mother and Muslim father. He gradually told me that two incidents in his teens suggested that he was under some kind of peculiar protection.

The first incident occurred when he and a friend wandered with their goats into Turkey and were accosted by three armed men who had them dig their own graves. Suddenly, two of the men turned their guns on their leader and allowed them to escape. A little while later, a fortune teller was entertaining Nazmi's family but complained that he could not perform for Nazmi himself.

It appears that Nazmi's parents nominal approach to their different religions left him confused but untroubled until he met an American Christian in a cafe who gave him a Turkish Bible in which he underlined John 6v45 “I tell you the truth, he who believes has everlasting life.” Nazmi received a reprimand from his father when he showed this to his parents. He went into his bedroom, threw the Bible at the wall and it fell open on his bed at this passage. In his frustration, Nazmi fell on his knees and prayed that he would wait until God showed him the truth.

Allow me to repeat what Nazmi told me happened next: “I found myself in a deep valley, threatened by a lion who I instinctively knew was Satan. I fended him off with a stout wooden staff. As I backed away up some stairs behind me to a level place, the lion followed but suddenly cowered and I turned to see Jesus Christ with a multitude of people in front of a glorious city. Jesus beckoned me in our gentle Eastern way with fingers down and bid me sit before Him. He told me he was sending me back to serve Him on Earth then I woke up in my room.

“I was so excited and shared my dream with my parents. My father was furious and threw me out of our home. My mother found me and said I could return but must never mention Jesus again. I found the American and we reasoned that I would be in danger of my life if my father put my story about. The American then arranged and financed my escape, first to help in a Christian bookshop in Istanbul that had connections with the Bible College of Wales, then he moved me on to the college itself.”

Nazmi sat by me at lectures during which I printed for him, the simplest possible summary of what was being said. The Holy Spirit gave him a remarkably rapid understanding of both lectures and English. During our quiet times, he would meditate on just a verse or two of scripture then share profound insights to encourage both of us in our Saviour and Lord Jesus Christ. He had clearly searched the scriptures before ever coming to the college and was an inspiration to me.

Nazmi had a clear premonition that he would eventually return to his homeland and give his life for the Lord. He did return to Istanbul and we kept in touch for a while. He married then, sadly, we lost touch.

The Adhesive Nature of Sin

Here's a personal anecdote to underline the effectiveness of Christ's shed blood to cleanse away our confessed sins.

My mowing machine threw a stone smashing a potting shed window. Just then a storm was approaching. I secured a sheet of PVC over the broken window, unwisely using tar-based tape over the PVC and 'around the corner' onto adjacent windows.

After the window was replaced I found that the tape that I had used had extremely strong adhesive which needed several coats of an acid based cleanser before the windows were clean.

Hymn: "What can wash away my sin? Nothing but the blood of Jesus", blood being selected by God as 'cleansing agent' – "Life being in the blood".

This illustrates the sublime mystery of the connection between Christ's blood, that was spilt on the cross, and its cleansing of our sins.

1 John 1v7: But if we walk in the light, as He is in the light, we have fellowship with one another, and the blood of Jesus, His Son, purifies us from all sin.

1 John 1v9: If we confess our sins, He is faithful and just and will forgive us our sins and purify us from all unrighteousness.

4. Who has the power to guide me safely through this journey from death to life?

Answer: Our Lord Jesus Christ himself who declares "***I AM*** *the way and the truth and the life. No-one comes to the father except through me.*" John14v6. Look at the cross of Christ and experience His peace. He has the power to guide us through all this.

By way of illustration, some 3500 years ago, the great Moses led Israel out of captivity. He saved many lives and foretold the coming of Christ through the following incident:

(photo © Jules & Jenny. “Sibthorpe, St Peter's church, east window detail” used under licence CC BY 2.0)

The John 3 story in verses 1-21, has Jesus referring to the Jewish High Priest Nicodemus back to the time when God judged rebellious Israel using a plague of poisonous snakes. To save themselves, they had only to look at a bronze serpent that Moses had mounted high on a pole. If they did so, God immediately saved them from the poison of the snake bites. The story perfectly illustrates the saving power of His own, future, sacrifice on the cross to save us from judgment for our own sins – of having fallen short of the glory of God.

That passage encourages us to **look** at **Jesus, the author and finisher of our faith** "For the joy that was set before him he endured the cross, scorning its shame, and sat down at the right hand of the throne of God." (Hebrews 12v2)

Here is the best known verse in the Bible: John 3v16: "For God so loved the world that He gave His one and only Son, that whoever believes in Him shall not perish but have eternal life."

Then comes the alternative in verse 18 "but whoever does not believe stands condemned already because they have not believed in the name of God's one and only Son."

Be encouraged to read the verses 1-21 from John 3 which is provided for you in full in the addendum at the end of this book.

5. Can one know Jesus personally as compared to just knowing about him?

ANSWER: Jesus said "***I AM*** *the gate for the sheep – whoever enters through me will be saved*" John10v7-9.

Westminster Street Sweeper

I was once working for a time at the Government Department of Trade and Industry offices at Westminster. As I passed a workman I heard him singing about Jesus "You ask me how I know He lives, He lives within my heart". This would draw the attention of passing, pin-stripe suited officials who would occasionally stop to enquire about that song. The workman explained that he had become a Christian believer and was able to rejoice in his newfound faith that his sins were forgiven and that he was looking forward to eternity in heaven with Christ. He had experienced what it is to be Born Again and be part of God's Kingdom on Earth and the Christian church.

The Apostle Paul, visualising Roman armour, tells us in Ephesians 6v12-17 that "our struggle is not against flesh and blood but against the rulers, the authorities, the powers of this dark world and against the spiritual forces of evil in the heavenly realms." We should therefore "Put on the whole armour of God comprising the belt of truth, the breastplate of righteousness, the sandals of peace. In addition we need to take up the shield of faith to extinguish the flaming arrows of the evil one (temptation), and put on the helmet of salvation and the sword of the Spirit which is the word of God."

How urgent is it for me to make my peace with God?

Best do it NOW or else you will delay experiencing the joy of assurance and safety in Christ.

The following anecdote about an old friend, Rattray Sutherland, illustrates the awesome possibility of delay but also God's grace towards turning to God at the last minute:

The Rattray Sutherland Story: A View Over the Hill

Photo shows Rattray between friends.

It’s a privilege indeed to catch a view that takes one’s breath away. It’s even more unusual to catch a glimpse of heaven, of “angels rejoicing”.

I believe this is what happened one day at the Royal Marsden Hospital in 1973. Suddenly, patients in isolation wards rang for attention. When the nurses arrived, each of the patients asked the same question, “What is happening? There is something happening!” In their isolation, they were not to know of the touching scene taking place in another ward down their corridor. There, a great friend of mine, was making his peace with God.

His name was Rattray Sutherland. Until a few days earlier, he hadn’t been spiritually minded. Now, he was about to pass away after just three weeks of leukaemia. For some evenings previous, a Christian friend and I had chatted with Rattray through his intercom, with visual contact through a large window in his ward door.

We three had worked together overseas. We reminisced, and chatted about a book which the hospital had sterilised so Rattray could read it. The book was about how God forgives our sin when we believe that Christ paid for them on our behalf on the cross. Both Rattray and I knew we had much to be forgiven. He knew that I had accepted this pardon but could not see how God could forgive him “at the last minute.”

Soon, he was so ill that only his wife Anne could visit him. It was during one of these visits that the other patients sensed an extraordinary presence. Just at the moment when Rattray felt that he wanted, after all, to make his peace with God, a priest made a totally unscheduled visit to the hospital. While Rattray received God's forgiveness the other patients rang their bells.

I began this account by saying that this incident provided a glimpse into heaven. If we look up Luke 15v10 in the Bible, we read, "...I tell you, there is rejoicing in the presence of the angels of God over one sinner who repents." I believe that at that moment, everyone in those adjacent wards sensed the joy and peace of the angels reaching them from heaven.

6. What would be expected of me in following Jesus?

Answer: Feed your faith on Him – in John 6v35 Jesus declared "***I AM*** *the bread of life. He who comes to me will never go hungry, and he who believes in me will never be thirsty*".

Here is the Apostles Creed. The Apostles were the first twelve who Jesus sent to spread His good news. The Creed being a statement of the truth which the subsequent members of His church are to believe.

> "I believe in God, the Father almighty,
> creator of heaven and earth.
>
> I believe in Jesus Christ, his only Son, our Lord,
> who was conceived by the Holy Spirit,
> born of the Virgin Mary,
> suffered under Pontius Pilate,
> was crucified, died, and was buried;
> he descended to the dead.
> On the third day he rose again;

he ascended into heaven,
he is seated at the right hand of the Father,
and he will come to judge the living and the dead.

I believe in the Holy Spirit,
the holy catholic Church [the universal church],
the communion of saints,
the forgiveness of sins, the resurrection of the body,
and the life everlasting.
Amen."

And also "Ask the Holy Spirit for the Christ-like characteristics as listed in Galatians 5 and "Abide" in Him to produce fruit for His church and kingdom on Earth as encouraged in John 15.

Having faith to pray for the eternal safety of a friend

Here is a personal, poignant story:

This photo of John and I, in Uganda in the early 1960s, was taken when we both worked for Caltex Oil company.

According to our sister Jessie, our brother John at the age of 14, had repented of his sins and invited Jesus Christ into his life as Lord and Saviour. Subsequently however, he lacked peer support in such matters and his interest in following Christ fell away. The fact was that John's early adulthood was within the environment of our parents' missionary work among Africans. His sparkling personality soon drew him into the neighbouring European partying society which had little time for things spiritual.

Much later, John became ill while working in Saudi Arabia. On his return to the UK, his health rapidly deteriorated culminating in a coma in Tunbridge Wells Hospital. I visited him there during the evening before he died and endeavoured to comfort him with words of assurance of God's eternal love for him. He was unresponsive but curiously became aroused when I repeated my encouragement in Kiswahili – the language we had known as children. He passed away that night.

Subsequently, I experienced some assurance of John's eternal safety in

1. Remembering how Jesus forgave the sins of a paralytic because of the faith of his friends – like me (When Jesus saw their faith, he said, "Friend, your sins are forgiven." – Luke 5v20).

2. Remembering how in Genesis 19v1&16, God sent angels who grasped the hands of Lot and led him to safety for the Lord was merciful. **It was as that passage of scripture came to mind that the telephone rang from the hospital to say that John had just passed away.**

In the Gospel of John 6v37-40, Jesus promises "*Whoever comes to me I will never drive away. I shall lose none of all that my Father God has given me, but raise them up at the last day. For my Father's will is that everyone who looks to the Son and believes in him shall have eternal life, and I will raise him up at the last day."* Also, in verse 47, "*I tell you the truth, he who believes has everlasting life.*"

Later in John 11, before raising Lazarus from his grave, Jesus said "*I am the resurrection and the life. He who believes in me will live, even though he dies; and whoever lives and believes in me will never die.*"

7. How would I maintain this new, personal faith?

Answer: Jesus said "***I AM*** *the light of the world. Whoever follows me will never walk in darkness, but will have the light of life*" John 8v12. We are also reminded in Ephesians 4v25, that we, God's church/kingdom on Earth, are "All members of one body".

Join a Christian church where you can enjoy serving in the fellowship, worship and prayer and where you receive regular Bible teaching. In gentle and appropriate ways, begin to mention your joy in Jesus to folk who are not so blessed. Maintain your personal, daily quiet times with the Lord in Bible meditation, listening, and prayer.

Suggestions:

- Thank God in a simple prayer, for the work of His hands in creating the glory of the heavens and the beauty of the skies.
- If you have not already got one, obtain a Bible. You can obtain one free – with help from 'Good News for Everyone'. Start reading the Gospel of

John and especially the third chapter. For daily encouragement, dial up **'YouVersion' Bible app or 'Olive Tree Bible' app** in your app store. Ask for God the Holy Spirit to help you. God has promised that if you "ask and it will be given to you; seek and you will find; knock and the door will be opened to you." Luke 11v9-10. **You can also apply to Crusade for World Revival (CWR) for FREE Daily Bible Reading Notes.**

- God's motive is that He loves mankind so much that He sent His only Son Jesus Christ to die for our sins and that by believing this, we are forgiven and have eternal life.

Be sure to "Keep your accounts short" with The Lord by daily considering whether you have failings to confess to Him, being assured of His promise to forgive you and cleanse you from all unrighteousness through the blood of Jesus shed for you.

Prayer

The greatest privilege of a Christian is to talk to and listen to God, our father who has promised to never leave us nor forsake us, through His words in the Bible. The Holy Spirit is with us to guide our thoughts and actions in life through the wisdom of the Scriptures, which one can find incredibly relevant in our day to day lives. We can be encouraged to sit silently as we listen to what God might say into our heart (Psalm 46).

Here is a personal anecdote, involving two photos, to remind us that…

“Our unconfessed sins will surely find us out!”

Cocky young salesman – David Dare

Result of swerving to avoid a cyclist suddenly emerging from a village

As a twenty year old using a Mercedes company car, the first photo shows a very cocky young salesman (myself) temporarily using another employee's company car. That colleague had threatened me with dire consequences if I returned it with as much as a scratch.

Shortly afterwards I swerved to avoid a cyclist suddenly emerging from a village straight across my path. To avoid him my steering wheels were caught in a grader track which headed off into a swamp.

The second photograph shows interested spectators before I was rescued by the friendly owner of a Land Rover who hauled me back onto the road and on my way.

I never mentioned the incident to the owner until he saw it in my photo album twenty years later! There had been one scratch on the driver's door which I had hidden with a paint 'touch-up' stick.

Scriptural addendums

Firstly, the following commentary in which Jesus teaches about being Born Again.

John 3v1-21

[1] Now there was a Pharisee, a man named Nicodemus who was a member of the Jewish ruling council. [2] He came to Jesus at night and said, 'Rabbi, we know that you are a teacher who has come from God. For no one could perform the signs you are doing if God were not with him.'

[3] Jesus replied, 'Very truly I tell you, no one can see the kingdom of God unless they are born again.'

[4] 'How can someone be born when they are old?' Nicodemus asked. 'Surely they cannot enter a second time into their mother's womb to be born!'

[5] Jesus answered, 'Very truly I tell you, no one can enter the kingdom of God unless they are born of water and the Spirit. [6] Flesh gives birth to flesh, but the

Spirit gives birth to spirit. [7] You should not be surprised at my saying, "You must be born again." [8] The wind blows wherever it pleases. You hear its sound, but you cannot tell where it comes from or where it is going. So it is with everyone born of the Spirit.'

[9] 'How can this be?' Nicodemus asked.

[10] 'You are Israel's teacher,' said Jesus, 'and do you not understand these things? [11] Very truly I tell you, we speak of what we know, and we testify to what we have seen, but still you people do not accept our testimony. [12] I have spoken to you of earthly things and you do not believe; how then will you believe if I speak of heavenly things? [13] No one has ever gone into heaven except the one who came from heaven – the Son of Man. [14] Just as Moses lifted up the snake in the wilderness, so the Son of Man must be lifted up, [15] that everyone who believes may have eternal life in him.'

[16] For God so loved the world that he gave his one and only Son, that whoever believes in him shall not perish but have eternal life. [17] For God did not send his Son into the world to condemn the world, but to save the world through him. [18] Whoever believes in him is not condemned, but whoever does not believe stands condemned already because they have not believed in the name of God's one and only Son. [19] This is the verdict: light has come into the world, but people loved darkness instead of light because their deeds were evil. [20] Everyone who does evil hates the light, and will not come into the light for fear that their deeds will be exposed. [21] But whoever lives by the truth comes into the light, so that it may be seen plainly that what they have done has been done in the sight of God.

Secondly, a reminder that we are "Saved to serve"

Matthew 25v31-46

[31] 'When the Son of Man comes in his glory, and all the angels with him, he will sit on his glorious throne. [32] All the nations will be gathered before him, and he will separate the people one from another as a shepherd separates the sheep from the goats. [33] He will put the sheep on his right and the goats on his left.

[34] 'Then the King will say to those on his right, "Come, you who are blessed by my Father; take your inheritance, the kingdom prepared for you since the creation of the world. [35] For I was hungry and you gave me something to eat, I was thirsty and you gave me something to drink, I was a stranger and you invited me in, [36] I needed clothes and you clothed me, I was ill and you looked after me, I was in prison and you came to visit me."

[37] 'Then the righteous will answer him, "Lord, when did we see you hungry and feed you, or thirsty and give you something to drink? [38] When did we see you a stranger and invite you in, or needing clothes and clothe you? [39] When did we see you ill or in prison and go to visit you?"

[40] 'The King will reply, "Truly I tell you, whatever you did for one of the least of these brothers and sisters of mine, you did for me."

[41] 'Then he will say to those on his left, "Depart from me, you who are cursed, into the eternal fire prepared for the devil and his angels. [42] For I was hungry and you gave me nothing to eat, I was thirsty and you gave me nothing to drink, [43] I

was a stranger and you did not invite me in, I needed clothes and you did not clothe me, I was ill and in prison and you did not look after me.”

[44] ‘They also will answer, “Lord, when did we see you hungry or thirsty or a stranger or needing clothes or ill or in prison, and did not help you?”

[45] ‘He will reply, “Truly I tell you, whatever you did not do for one of the least of these, you did not do for me.”

[46] ‘Then they will go away to eternal punishment, but the righteous to eternal life.’

Finally – God’s promise of our, personal resurrection, as we believe in Jesus:

John 6v39-40

[39] And this is the will of him who sent me, that I shall lose none of all those he has given me, but raise them up at the last day. [40] For my Father’s will is that everyone who looks to the Son and believes in him shall have eternal life, and I will raise them up at the last day.’

Lightning Source UK Ltd.
Milton Keynes UK
UKHW021114040322
399573UK00005B/146

9 780992 757021